LAUNCH PAD
LIBRARY

MY AMAZING BODY

RACHEL WRIGHT

STAMPLEY

How to Use This Book

Cross references
Above some of the chapter titles, you will find a list of other chapters in the book that are related to the topic. Turn to these pages to find out more about each subject.

See for yourself
See-for-yourself bubbles give you the chance to test out some of the ideas in this book. They explain what you will need and what you have to do to see if an idea really works.

Quiz corner
In the quiz corner, you will find a list of questions. The answers to the quiz questions are somewhere in the same chapter. Try to answer all the questions about each subject.

Chatterboxes
Chatterboxes give you interesting facts about other things that are related to the subject.

Glossary
Difficult words are explained in the glossary on page 31. These words are in **bold** type in the book. Look them up in the glossary to find out what they mean.

Index
The index is on page 32. It is a list of important words mentioned in the book, with page numbers next to the entries. If you want to read about a subject, look it up in the index, then turn to the page number given.

Contents

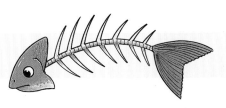

Your Amazing Body

Your body is an amazing machine. It can move, think, listen and talk. It also mends itself, changes shape and grows. Your body is made of lots of different parts, all working together. You can see some parts, such as your skin and hair. Others, such as your **brain** and **bones,** are hidden inside you.

Before you were born
You started your life inside your mother's body. At first you were just a tiny speck, smaller than a dot. Then you grew and grew. Finally you were ready to be born.

◀ It takes forty weeks for a baby to grow inside its mother's body. Then the baby is ready to be born.

Growing up
When you grew from a baby into a toddler, your body changed quickly. You grew about eight inches a year. You are still growing and changing now, but much more slowly. At seven years old, you grow nearly three inches taller each year. When you are a teenager, your body will start to grow and change faster again.

Growing older

Many people stay healthy all through their adult years. They take care of their bodies by staying in shape, eating well and taking time to relax.

▼ Older adults often spend time doing the things they enjoy most, such as playing with grandchildren.

▲ As you grow, your body gets stronger and you can run faster.

Teenagers

Between the ages of about ten and fourteen, your body will grow taller and change shape. By the time you are about twenty, you will be fully grown.

As girls grow up, they become more rounded, like their mothers. Boys develop broader shoulders and their voices get deeper. Both girls and boys become hairier as they grow older.

Quiz Corner

● What happens to your body between the ages of ten and fourteen?

● At about what age are you fully grown?

● What happens to a boy's voice as he grows older?

● How can you stay healthy all your life?

look at: Muscles, page 8; Breathing, page 12

Skeleton

Inside your body there is a strong framework of 206 **bones** called a skeleton. Your skeleton gives your body its shape and strength. If you did not have a skeleton, you would be as floppy as a beanbag. Your skeleton also helps protect the fragile parts of your body.

▼ Some of the bones in your skeleton are tiny. Others are large and strong.

· · · · · skull

· · · · · · · ribs

· · · · · backbone or spine

· · · · · thighbones

· · · · · knee

· · · · · · · ankle

Inside your bones

Your bones are not dead and dried up. They are alive, just like the rest of you. Your bones are hard and solid on the outside, but inside many of them have a fatty jelly called bone marrow. Bone marrow helps make **blood**.

bone

marrow

CHATTERBOX

Insects and crabs do not have skeletons inside their bodies. Instead they have hard outer shells, called exoskeletons, to protect their soft insides.

Skull and rib cage
Each bone in your body has a special job. Your skull is a bony helmet that protects your **brain**. Your ribs make a cage around your **heart** and **lungs**, which are soft and could be hurt easily.

Joints

Wherever bones meet in your skeleton, you have a joint. Your knees are hinge joints. They let you bend and straighten your legs. Your shoulders are ball-and-socket joints. They let you move your arms in circles.

▼ You can bend, twist and turn your body because you have joints between your bones.

▲ Your spine is flexible because it is made up of lots of little bones and joints.

Broken bones

If you break a bone, new bone grows to join the broken ends together. A hard bandage called a cast helps keep the bone straight while it mends.

Quiz Corner

- Which part of your skeleton protects your heart?
- What kind of joint is your hip joint?
- What is another name for your backbone?

Finger joints are called knuckles.

Shoulders are ball-and-socket joints.

Elbows are hinge joints.

......Hips are ball-and-socket joints.

........Knees are hinge joints.

Toes have hinge joints.

7

look at: Brain, page 16; Skeleton, page 6

Muscles

Muscles make your body move. Many of your muscles are attached to the **bones** of your skeleton by strong straps called tendons. Every time you run, jump or walk, lots of muscles pull on your bones. This makes your bones move, which makes your body move.

▼ Your muscles will stay healthy and strong if you make them work hard by playing energetic games.

Pairs of muscles
Many of your muscles work in pairs. One muscle pulls a bone one way, then its partner pulls the bone back again.

When you bend your elbow, your biceps muscle becomes shorter, pulling your arm up.

biceps

triceps

When you straighten your arm, your triceps muscle becomes shorter, pulling your arm down.

Sending messages
Your **brain** controls your muscles. It figures out which muscles you need to move each part of your body. Your brain sends your muscles messages to pull on your bones. Then, when your muscles have pulled, they send messages back to your brain.

8

Making faces

Not all your muscles pull on bones. Some of the muscles in your face pull on your skin. You use these muscles every time you smile, frown, or make a funny face.

▲ Every time you frown, your body uses more than forty muscles. A smile uses only about fifteen muscles. So if you want to save muscle power — smile!

Different muscles

You have three different types of muscles in your body. Each type has a different job. One type pulls your bones to make you move. Another type pushes your food through your body. A third type makes your heart beat.

Quiz Corner

- What do muscles help you do?
- Why are energetic games good for you?
- How many different types of muscles are there in your body?
- Which uses more muscles, a smile or a frown?

9

look at: Blood, page 14; Taking Care of Yourself, page 28

Eating

Your body needs food to help it grow and work properly. But your body cannot use the food you eat just as it is. Food has to be chopped up and chewed, then changed inside you to a form which can pass into your **blood**. Your blood can then carry it to all the different parts of your body.

Esophagus and intestines
Inside your body, long tubes connect your mouth to your stomach and your stomach to your bottom. The first tube (esophagus) is fairly straight, but the lower tubes (intestines) are wiggly. Different things happen to your food as it travels through these.

◀ Your body takes all the goodness it needs from your food, then it pushes out the **waste**.

CHATTERBOX

Snakes don't chew their food the way you do. When an egg-eating snake spies a tasty-looking egg, it opens its mouth wide and swallows it whole.

Healthy eating

You need to eat small amounts of lots of different kinds of foods to give you **energy** and help you grow. Eggs, meat and fish all help you grow. Bread and pasta give you energy. Fruit and vegetables are full of **vitamins and minerals**.

....*When you chew, your teeth chop up your food and your saliva makes it soft enough for you to swallow.*

....*After you swallow, your food is pushed down your esophagus and into your stomach.*

....*Inside your stomach, your food is broken down by strong juices and turned into a thick, soupy mush.*

....*By now, the useful nutrients of your food are ready. They pass through the sides of your intestines into nearby blood vessels.*

....*Any pieces of food that your body cannot use are squeezed along to the end of your intestines as waste. You push them out of your body when you go to the toilet.*

▼ Babies do not have any teeth to chew their food, so baby food is usually soft and easy to swallow.

◄ Your body is mostly made up of water. Every day, you need to drink fresh water to stay healthy. Your body tells you when to drink by making you feel thirsty.

Quiz Corner

● Why do you need to eat?

● What happens to food in your stomach?

● Which foods give you energy?

● When do you feel thirsty?

● Why is baby food soft?

11

look at: Blood, page 14

Breathing

You need to breathe to stay alive. When you breathe in, you suck air into your body through your nose or mouth. The air goes down your windpipe, then into your **lungs**. Your lungs are stretchy bags that fill up with air, in the same way as a sponge fills with water.

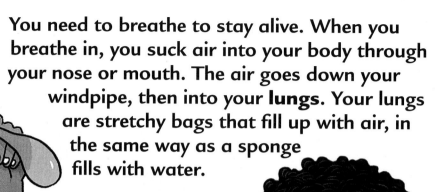

▲ When you breathe in, your lungs get bigger as they fill up with air.

Breathing in

In the air, there is an invisible gas called **oxygen**. Every time you take a breath, oxygen goes into your lungs. Inside your lungs, oxygen seeps into your **blood vessels**. Then your **blood** carries the oxygen all around your body.

▲ When you breathe out, your lungs get smaller as you push out the air. This air can blow up a balloon.

SEE FOR YOURSELF

When you breathe in, your chest gets bigger to make room for your lungs. When you breathe out, your chest gets smaller again. Cross your arms like this and take a deep breath in and out. You should be able to feel your chest moving.

Breathing out

As your body uses up oxygen, it makes a gas called **carbon dioxide**. This gas is a **waste** product, which means your body does not need it. Your blood carries this gas back to your lungs so that you can breathe it out. All day and night, you breathe in oxygen and breathe out carbon dioxide.

▼ Fish can breathe underwater, but people cannot. Scuba divers carry tanks of compressed air on their backs for breathing underwater.

Quiz Corner

● What is oxygen?

● How does oxygen get into your body?

● What happens to your chest as you breathe in and out?

● How do divers breathe underwater?

look at: Muscles, page 8; Eating, page 10; Breathing, page 12

Blood

▼ **Your heart pumps blood through your blood vessels.**

Blood is a thick liquid that flows around and around in your body. It carries goodness from the food you eat and **oxygen** from the air you breathe to every part of your body. It also picks up **waste** and takes it to parts of your body that can get rid of it.

Blood vessels

Blood travels through your body in flexible tubes called **blood vessels**. Blood vessels run from your **heart** to your **lungs**, then all the way around your body and back again. Sometimes you can see your blood vessels through your skin. They look like thin blue lines.

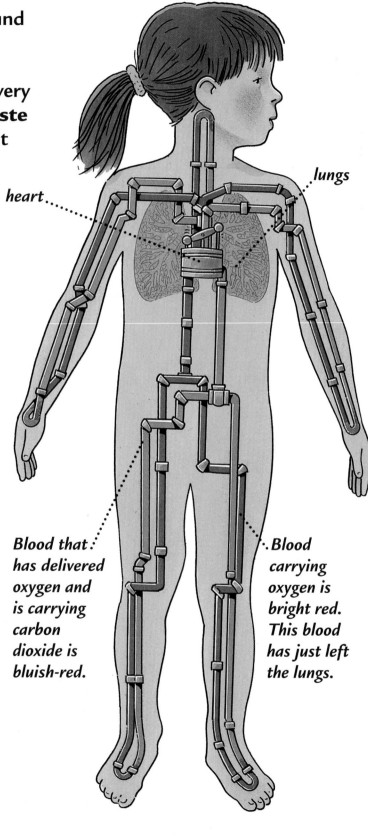

heart

lungs

Blood that has delivered oxygen and is carrying carbon dioxide is bluish-red.

Blood carrying oxygen is bright red. This blood has just left the lungs.

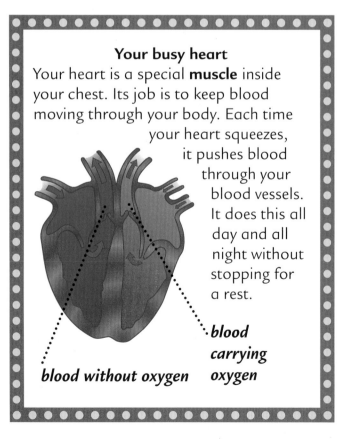

Your busy heart
Your heart is a special **muscle** inside your chest. Its job is to keep blood moving through your body. Each time your heart squeezes, it pushes blood through your blood vessels. It does this all day and all night without stopping for a rest.

blood carrying oxygen

blood without oxygen

14

New skin

If you cut yourself, thick blood plugs up the hole. Over time, the plug hardens to make a scab. New skin grows under the scab, then the scab falls off.

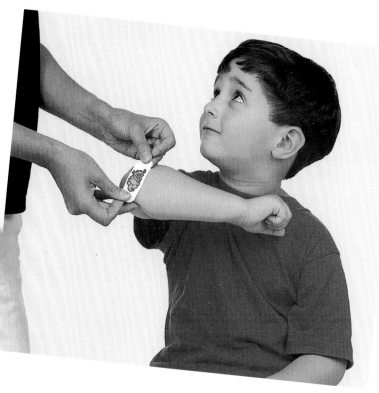

▲ A plaster or bandage helps keep germs from getting into your body through a cut. It keeps the cut clean until the skin heals.

CHATTERBOX

If you stretched out all the blood vessels in your body and laid them end to end, they would be almost long enough to go around the Earth three times.

Quiz Corner

● Name three things that blood does.

● What color is blood with oxygen in it?

● What does your heart do all day and night?

● What happens when you cut yourself?

Fighting germs

Your blood also helps your body fight **germs**. Germs are tiny living things that can make you sick when they live inside your body. Special cells in your blood, called **white blood cells**, fight these harmful germs and help to make you well again.

look at: Muscles, page 8; Breathing, page 12; Hearing, page 18; Seeing, page 20; Touching, page 24

Brain

Inside your head, there is a soft pinkish-gray lump protected by your skull. This is your **brain**. Your brain controls your whole body. It tells your **muscles** and **senses** what to do. It also does all your thinking, learning and remembering.

Network of nerves

Your brain is linked to every part of your body by pathways called **nerves**. Your brain sends messages all over your body along these pathways. Different parts of your body also use this network to send messages to your brain.

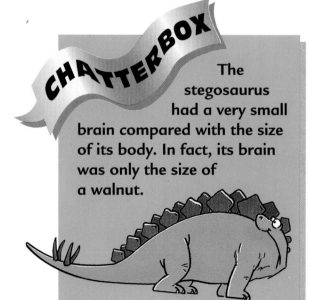

CHATTERBOX

The stegosaurus had a very small brain compared with the size of its body. In fact, its brain was only the size of a walnut.

▲ This is what the outer layer of your brain looks like. Different parts of your outer brain do different jobs.

*This part of your brain sends nerve messages to your muscles. It tells them to pull on your **bones** so that you move.*

This part of your brain controls your speech. It helps you talk.

This part of your brain receives nerve messages from your eyes. Then it lets you know what you are seeing.

This part of your brain sorts out the nerve messages from your ears. It tells you what you are hearing.

Your brain stem controls things you do that you do not have to think about, such as breathing and sneezing.

Dreams

Your brain works all day and all night. Even when you are asleep, it controls your heartbeat and breathing. Your brain also keeps thinking while you sleep. Sometimes you remember these night thoughts as dreams.

▲ Dreams usually last for about half an hour. Most people have about four dreams each night, but they don't always remember them.

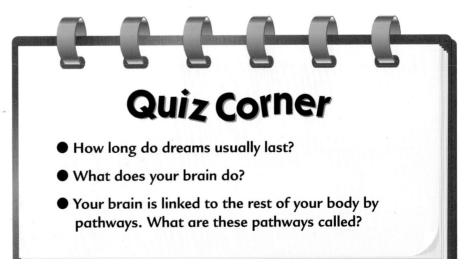

Quiz Corner

● How long do dreams usually last?

● What does your brain do?

● Your brain is linked to the rest of your body by pathways. What are these pathways called?

look at: Brain, page 16

Hearing

Hearing is one of your five main **senses**. The others are seeing, smelling, tasting and touching. Your sense of hearing lets you hear many different sounds, from a pin dropping to an elephant trumpeting. It lets you enjoy your favorite music. It can also warn you of many dangers that you cannot see, such as a car coming up behind you.

Looking at ears
The two flaps on the sides of your head are only part of your ears. The rest of your ears lies safely inside your head, protected by your hard, bony skull.

Inside your ears
Your ear flaps are similar to the wide end of a funnel. They catch sounds from the air which go into your ears. In your inner ear, the sounds are turned into messages. These messages whiz along **nerves** to your **brain**. Your brain then tells you what you are hearing.

brain

sound

inner ear

▲ Your brain sorts out the sounds you hear. You can tell the difference between all kinds of musical instruments.

CHATTERBOX

Many animals can wiggle their ears. This means that they can figure out where sounds are coming from without turning their heads and attracting attention.

Sign language

Many people who cannot hear learn to talk using special hand signs to spell or show different words and sentences. This way of talking is called signing.

▲ These children are talking by signing. The girl is saying that she is tired, and the boy wants to know what time it is.

Quiz Corner

● Why is hearing so useful?

● Which part of your body protects your inner ears?

● What can a rabbit do with its ears that people can't?

● How do people who cannot hear talk to each other?

19

look at: Brain, page 16

Seeing

Your eyes need light to work. When you look at something, light bouncing off that thing goes into your eyes through the small black holes in them. Messages about the light are sent along a **nerve** to your **brain**, which makes sense of what you see.

▼ Seeing is one of your five main **senses**. It is sometimes considered to be the most important one.

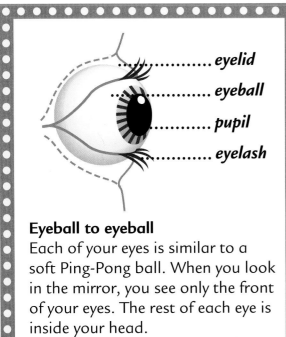

- eyelid
- eyeball
- pupil
- eyelash

Eyeball to eyeball
Each of your eyes is similar to a soft Ping-Pong ball. When you look in the mirror, you see only the front of your eyes. The rest of each eye is inside your head.

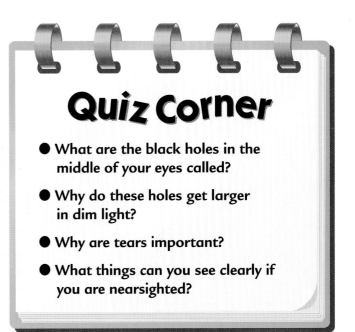

▼ Some people wear glasses to help them see clearly.

Letting in light
The black hole in the middle of each eye is called a pupil. In dim light, your pupils become bigger to let more light into your eyes. In bright light, your pupils shrink to protect your eyes.

Wearing glasses
Some people can see things clearly only if they are up close. These people are nearsighted. Others can see things clearly only if they are far away. They are farsighted. Wearing glasses can help correct these problems.

SEE FOR YOURSELF
Ask a friend to stand in a darkened room. Look at one of his pupils. Then turn on the light. His pupils will get smaller.

Keeping your eyes clean
Salty tears help to keep your eyes clean and wet. You also make tears when you feel unhappy, but nobody knows why.

Quiz Corner
- What are the black holes in the middle of your eyes called?
- Why do these holes get larger in dim light?
- Why are tears important?
- What things can you see clearly if you are nearsighted?

look at: Eating, page 10; Brain, page 16

Smelling and Tasting

Smelling and tasting are two of your **senses**. When you eat, your tongue picks up tastes and your nose picks up smells. These let you enjoy the full flavor of food. If your nose is blocked by a cold, smells cannot get into it. When this happens, you cannot taste properly.

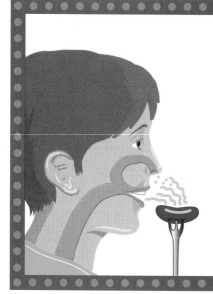

Inside your nose

Inside your head, the holes leading from your mouth and nose meet. When you eat, smells from your food go up the back of your mouth and into your nose. Inside your nose, smell collectors pick up these smells and send messages about them to your **brain**.

Smells in the air

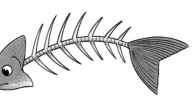

Your nose does not just help your tongue with tasting. It also picks up smells floating in the air. Smells are invisible, like the air. When you breathe in, they go up your nose.

▶ Your senses of taste and smell tell you if food is good or bad to eat. Fresh food tastes and smells delicious. Rotten food tastes and smells horrible.

Taste buds

Tiny bumps, called taste buds, cover your tongue. Taste buds at the front of your tongue pick up sweet and salty flavors. Those on the sides sense sour tastes, such as lemon. Those at the back pick up bitter tastes, such as coffee.

This part picks up sour tastes.

This part picks up sweet and salty tastes.

This part picks up bitter tastes.

SEE FOR YOURSELF

Try this test to see how much stronger your sense of smell is than your sense of taste. First, blindfold a friend. Then hold an onion under her nose and feed her some bread. Your friend will think she is eating an onion!

Quiz Corner

- Why can't you taste your food well when your nose is blocked?

- Which four kinds of flavors can you taste?

- Why are your senses of taste and smell useful?

look at: Brain, page 16; Skin, page 26

Touching

Your **sense** of touch lets you know how things feel against your skin. When you stroke something with your hand, **nerves** in your skin send messages about the feeling to your **brain**. If the feeling is painful or unfamiliar, your brain tells you to snatch your hand away. If the feeling is safe and soft, your brain lets you leave your hand where it is.

▶ Stroking the soft fur of a pet is a soothing feeling. So is hugging someone you love.

SEE FOR YOURSELF

Here is a way to test a friend's sense of touch. Make a hole in the side of a box and ask a friend to stick his hand through it. Then put different things — such as cold spaghetti, a potato and a leaf — inside the box. Can your friend guess what each thing is just by touching it?

Different feelings

Your sense of touch tells you if something is hot or cold, hard or soft, rough or smooth. It also lets you know if something is hurting you. Pain is useful because it lets you know when something is harming your body.

▲ Your sense of touch warns you if a drink is hot or cold. It also tells you if things are wet.

▲ When you step on a thumbtack, a sharp pain tells you to take your foot away.

▲ When you shake hands, you can feel your friend's hand pressing against yours.

◀ A pineapple's skin feels rough and hard, but an apple's skin feels smooth.

Tongue, lips and fingertips

Some parts of your skin feel things more clearly than others because they have more nerve endings. Your tongue, lips and fingertips have lots of nerve endings. This is why a baby often feels things with its mouth.

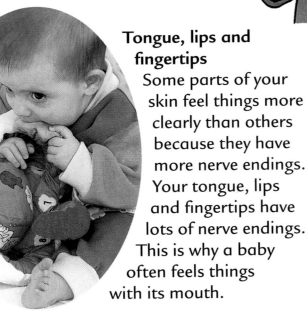

▲ Often, a baby finds out what shape a toy is by putting it in its mouth.

Quiz Corner

- Which part of your body feels things more clearly, the back of your hand or the tips of your fingers?
- Why is pain useful?
- Why does a baby often put things in its mouth?

25

look at: Touching, page 24

Skin

Your skin is like a stretchy, washable, waterproof suit that covers you from head to toe. It helps stop harmful things from getting into your body. It also works hard to keep you at the right **temperature**.

▶ Your skin keeps water from soaking into your body. It also keeps the inside of your body from drying out in the sun.

Skin color

Everyone's skin has a kind of dye, or color, called melanin. Melanin helps protect skin from the sun's harmful rays. People with dark skin have more melanin than people with fair skin. This means that dark skin is protected from the sun better than fair skin. In sunny weather, skin makes more melanin to protect itself. This is why your skin may become browner in the sun.

Sweat

Tiny holes called pores cover your skin. When you are very hot, salty water — sweat — comes out of the pores. As the sweat dries, it takes heat away from your skin. This helps cool you down.

CHATTERBOX

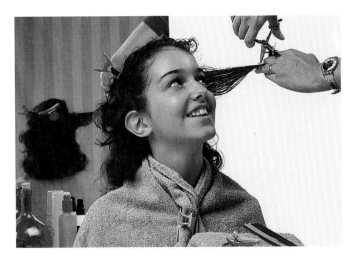

Reptiles, such as geckos and snakes, cannot sweat to keep cool. Instead, when they are hot, they lie in a shady spot until they cool down.

Save your skin

Too much sunshine can burn and damage your skin. If you want to have fun in the sun safely, follow these rules.

● Wear a wide-brimmed hat to protect your face.

● Use sunscreen on any parts of your body not covered by clothing.

Looking at hair

Hair grows all over your skin, except on your lips, the soles of your feet and the palms of your hands. In some places your hair is easy to see. In others, it is so fine, you have to look closely to find it.

▲ The hair on your head grows faster than the hair on the rest of your body.

Getting a haircut

The roots of your hair, which are inside your skin, are alive and growing. But the part of your hair that you can see is dead. This is why getting a haircut does not hurt.

Quiz Corner

● Why do you sweat when you are hot?

● How can you save your skin from sunburn?

● Which part of your hair is alive?

● Where does your hair not grow?

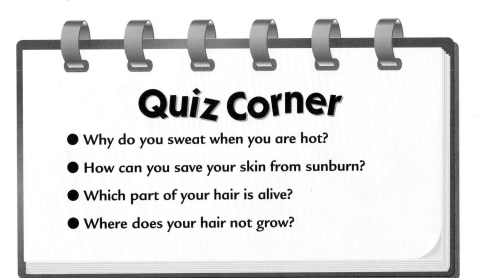

look at: Muscles, page 8; Eating, page 10

Taking Care of Yourself

There are lots of ways of taking care of yourself. Eating the right food is one way. Getting enough sleep and exercise are other ways. Washing your body, cleaning your teeth and combing your hair each day are important, too, because keeping clean makes you look, feel and smell healthy.

Sugar alert

Sugary foods and drinks are great for a treat and give you an instant boost of **energy**. But to keep healthy, you should eat a mixture of all the different types of foods, including plenty of fresh fruit and vegetables.

Adult teeth

At about the age of six, you start to lose your first set of teeth. One by one, your second set of teeth grows in their place. You have only one set of adult teeth, so make sure you take care of them.

Your front teeth are for biting and tearing food.

Your back teeth are for grinding and chewing food.

28

Keeping happy and healthy

Playing soccer, going for a walk, running and swimming are all types of exercise. Exercising regularly helps keep your body healthy and strong. It's lots of fun too.

Washing your hands

You should always wash your hands before eating or touching food. This stops any **germs** that might be on your hands from getting on your food and making you sick.

▲ Playing outside with friends is a good way to exercise.

◀ To wash yourself really well, you need to use soap and clean, warm water. The soap loosens the greasy dirt on your skin and the water washes it away.

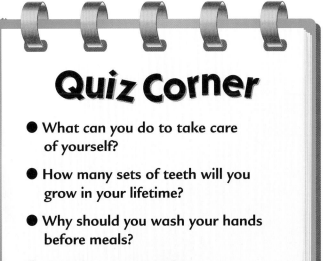

Quiz Corner

- What can you do to take care of yourself?

- How many sets of teeth will you grow in your lifetime?

- Why should you wash your hands before meals?

- How does soap work?

29

Amazing Facts

● The human ear can tell the difference between more than 1,500 different musical sounds.

☆ Every night you grow a little taller as the disks between the bones in your back spread out. During the day, the disks shrink and you become your usual height.

● Did you know that you blink about 20,000 times a day? Blinking helps wash dust and germs from your eyes.

☆ Your body sheds tiny flakes of skin all the time. Every year, you shed about half a pound of dead skin. House dust is partly made up of dead skin.

● Your hair grows faster in the morning than it does at night.

☆ Did you know that your bones are not the strongest material in your body? The tough outer covering on your teeth, called enamel, is stronger.

● The smallest bone in your body is in your ear. It is called the stirrup and is only about the size of a pea.

☆ You have about fourteen billion brain cells. These control everything that your body does.

● A sip of milk takes just six seconds to travel from your mouth to your stomach. Food takes up to twenty-four hours to pass through your body.

☆ When you sneeze, you force air out of your lungs at a speed of up to 100 miles per hour, faster than some hurricanes!

● Did you know that you have the same number of bones in your neck as a giraffe? Seven!

☆ The human body can stay alive for three weeks without food but only a few minutes without oxygen.

Glossary

blood A thick liquid that flows through your body. Blood is made up of watery fluid, red blood cells and **white blood cells.**

blood vessels Tubes that carry **blood** through your body.

bones The hard white parts of your skeleton, which gives your body shape.

brain The control center of your body.

carbon dioxide A **waste** gas your body makes when it uses **oxygen**. Your **blood** carries it to your **lungs** and you breathe it out.

cell A tiny living unit. All living things are made up of cells.

energy The strength to do things.

germ A tiny living thing that can make you sick.

heart The **muscle** that pumps **blood** through your body.

lungs Spongelike organs in your chest that process the air.

muscles Parts inside your body that help move your **bones** and help with things such as absorbing food and breathing.

nerves Passageways that carry messages to and from your **brain**.

oxygen A gas in the air. Oxygen goes into your **lungs** when you breathe in. Then it passes from your lungs into your **blood** and travels to all parts of your body.

senses The powers that make you aware of what is around you. Your five senses are seeing, hearing, touching, smelling and tasting.

temperature How hot or cold something is.

vitamins and minerals Substances found in food. You need them in order to stay healthy.

waste Something your body does not need.

white blood cells Parts of your **blood** that destroy **germs**.

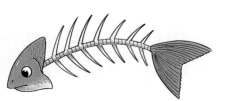

Index

Published in the USA by
C.D. Stampley Enterprises, Inc.,
Charlotte, NC, USA.
Created by Two-Can Publishing Ltd.,
London. English-language edition
© Two-Can Publishing Ltd, 1997

Text: Rachel Wright
Consultant: Dr. R. Ibrahim
Watercolor artwork: Stuart Trotter
Computer artwork: D Oliver
Commissioned photography:
Steve Gorton

Editorial Director: Jane Wilsher
Art Director: Carole Orbell
Production Director: Lorraine Estelle
Project Manager: Eljay Yildirim
Editors: Belinda Webber,
Deborah Kespert
Assistant Editors: Julia Hillyard,
Claire Yude
Co-edition Editor: Leila Peerun
Photo Research:
Dipika Palmer-Jenkins

ISBN: 0-915741-78-4

Photographic credits: Britstock-IFA
(Westock, David Perry) p11tr,
(Bernd Ducke) p18-19c; Steve Gorton
p7, p15, p17, p19br, p26, p27,
p28-29c; Images front cover; Pictor
International p22-23; Fiona Pragoff
p7, p8-9, p24; Reflections Photo
Library (Jennie Woodcock) p25bl;
Tony Stone Images p4-5, p5, p21,
p29tr; Telegraph Colour Library p20;
Zefa p11c, p13.

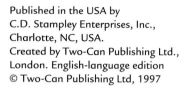
WRI
C.1
2000